RACHEL RODRÍGUEZ

BUILDING ON NATURE
THE LIFE OF ANTONI GAUDÍ

illustrated by JULIE PASCHKIS

HENRY HOLT AND COMPANY 🙟 New York

Henry Holt and Company, LLC
Publishers since 1866
175 Fifth Avenue
New York, New York 10010
www.HenryHoltKids.com

Library of Congress Cataloging-in-Publication Data
Rodríguez, Rachel.
Building on nature : the life of Antoni Gaudí / Rachel Rodríguez ; illustrated by Julie Paschkis.—1st ed.
p.   cm.
ISBN-13: 978-0-8050-8745-1 / ISBN-10: 0-8050-8745-1
1. Gaudí, Antoni, 1852–1926—Juvenile literature. 2. Architects—Spain—Biography—
Juvenile literature. 3. Picture books for children. I. Paschkis, Julie. II. Title.
NA1313.G3R63 2009
720.92—dc22   [B]   2008038213

First Edition—2009 / Designed by Linda Lockowitz
The artist used Winsor & Newton gouaches to create the illustrations in this book.
Printed in China on acid-free paper. ∞

1   3   5   7   9   10   8   6   4   2

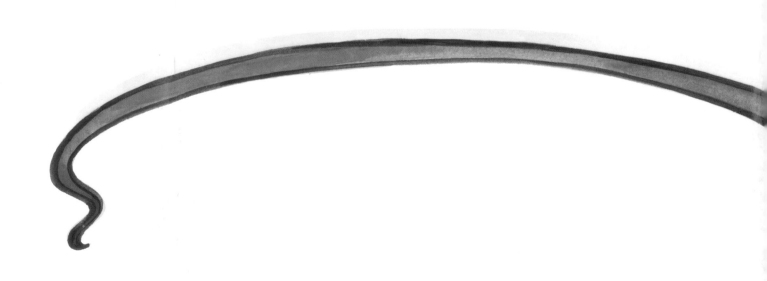

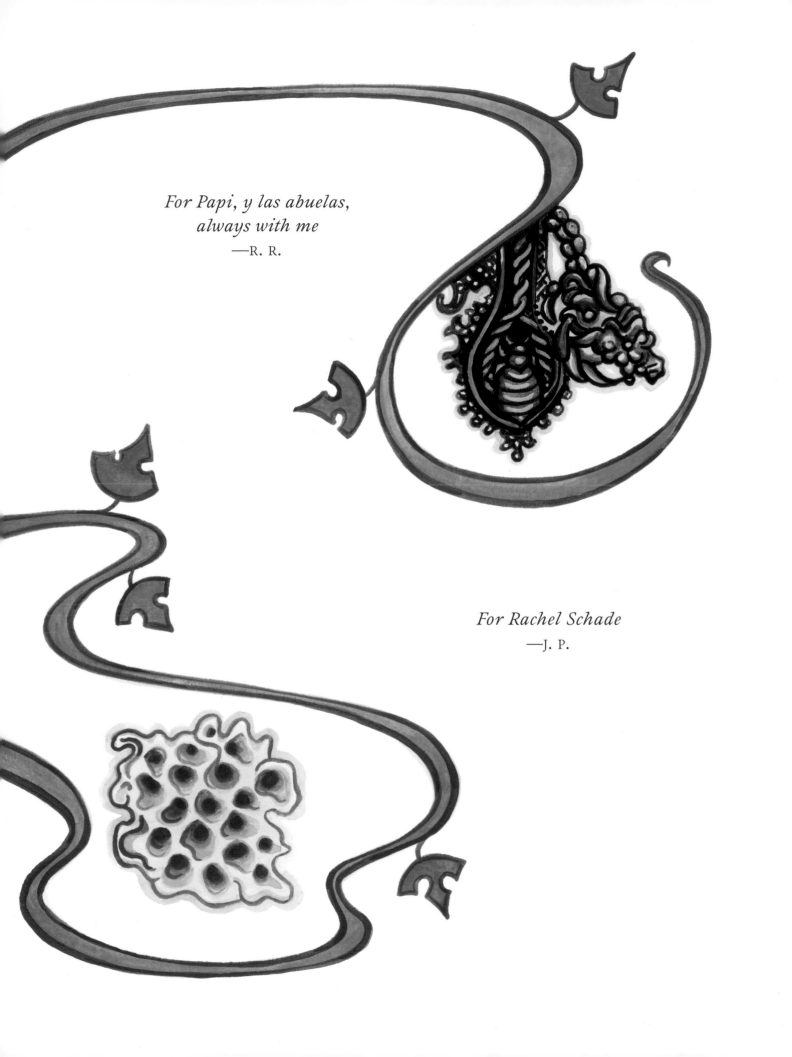

*For Papi, y las abuelas,
always with me*
—R. R.

For Rachel Schade
—J. P.

In a small village in Spain
lives a boy named Antoni Gaudí.

For him, the world is Catalonia.
Mountain peaks jag against the sky.
Silvery olive trees sway in the breeze.
The sea sparkles blue.

Little Gaudí often feels sick.
His bones and joints ache.
He can't always run and play
with his sister and brother.

But Gaudí has time to notice.
With wide eyes, he observes the world.
All around him is light, form, and
the Great Book of Nature.
He will read from it all his life.

Gaudí's father works with copper and fire.
His mother's family are metalsmiths, too.
Over and over, he watches flat pieces of metal
become shapes with a hollow space inside.

Gaudí grows stronger.

He makes friends with two boys.

Together, they explore an ancient monastery.

He dreams of rebuilding the ruins.

After high school, Gaudí goes to Barcelona to be an architect.

He studies important monuments
and reads at the library.
Other architects teach him.

Gaudí wears fine top hats and coats.
He attends the opera and goes to church, too.

He designs his own desk.
He creates lampposts for the city.

Soon others ask Gaudí
to build for them.

His first big project is the Vicens House.

Everywhere, zinnia tiles bloom.
The house is a checkerboard of color.
Passersby stop and stare.
They aren't used to Gaudí's bright colors.

Gaudí brings nature inside the house, too.

Leaves climb up walls.

Cherries hang overhead.

Birds wheel around and soar to the sky.

Gaudí works on several projects at once.
He begins to design the Holy Family Church.
For years, he will plan and dream it into life.
His faith inspires his work.

For Gaudí, building is serious. Everything must function. But he isn't afraid to use his imagination.

Each time visitors use a door knocker, they squash a bedbug underneath.

A peephole looks like a honeycomb.

Gaudí makes people notice his smallest creations.

He designs a gate for his friend
Güell's country home.
A dragon perches atop diamonds and squares,
baring his fangs and slithery tongue.
Gaudí's creations get braver.

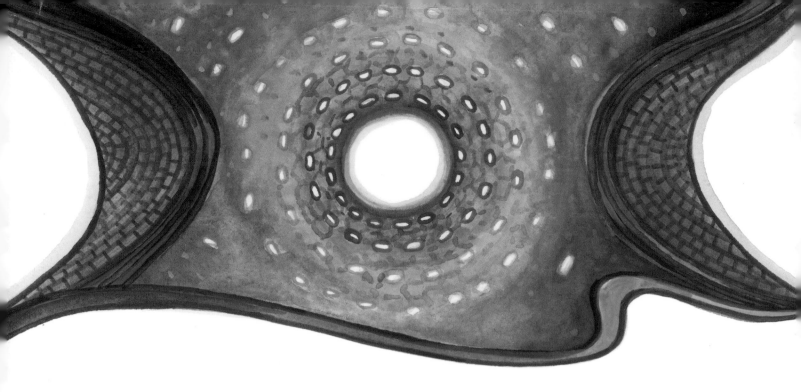

For Güell's Palace in town, Gaudí builds a curving ramp
to a basement stable. Horses clomp down to it.
Upstairs, sunlight enters a domed ceiling.
The family enjoys their salon beneath a starry sky.

How do you build a chapel underground?
Gaudí studies this giant problem for ten years.

He creates an upside-down model
that resembles a colony of bats.

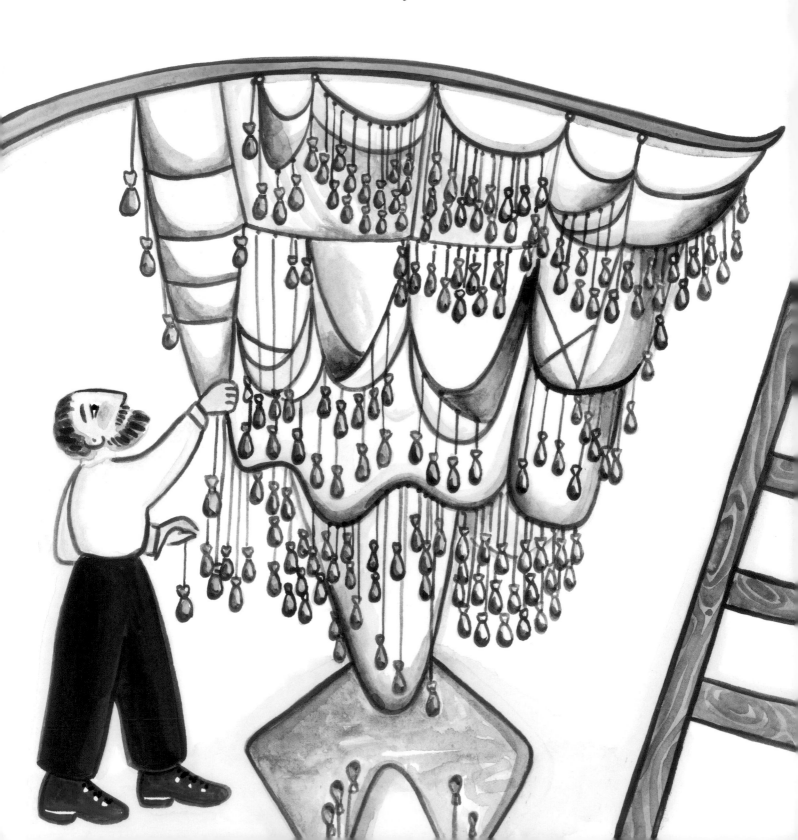

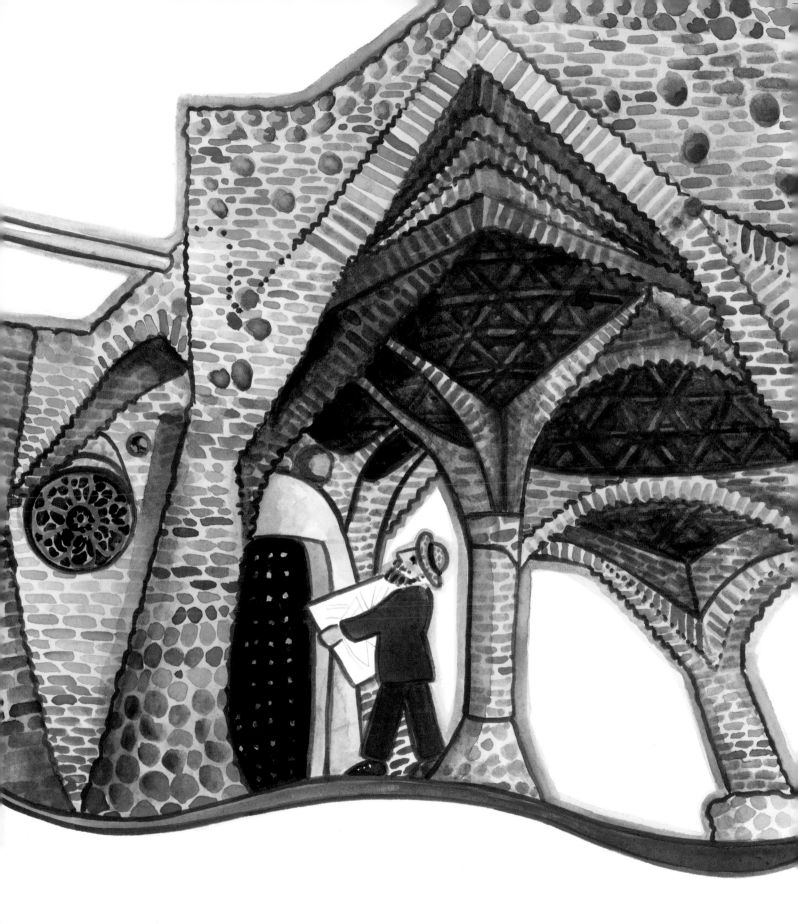

Gaudí learns how the arches and columns will work.
He turns it right side up and begins to build the Colonia Crypt.

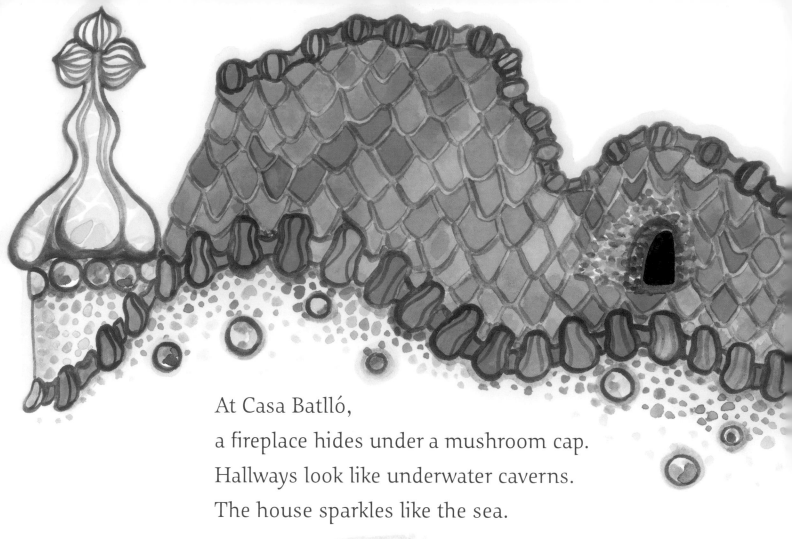

At Casa Batlló,
a fireplace hides under a mushroom cap.
Hallways look like underwater caverns.
The house sparkles like the sea.

The roof arches in a dragon's spine.
Pillars are giant animal feet, balconies are bones,

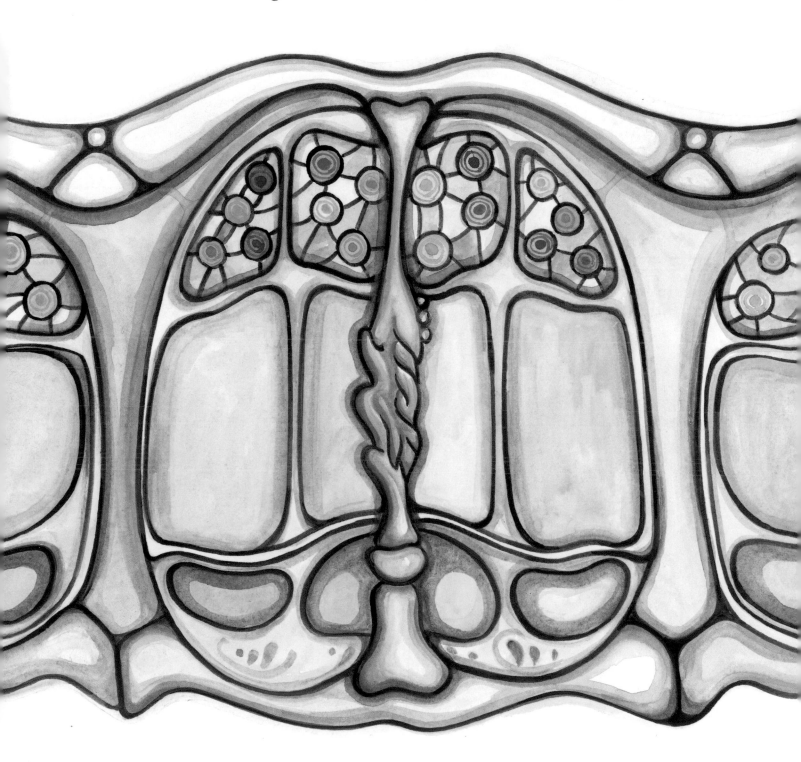

and round walls are smooth serpent skin.
A sword of a tower slays the beast.

Everyone gapes at Gaudí's grand twists of imagination.
But not everyone enjoys his strange buildings.
Gaudí pays no attention to the talk.
He listens to himself.

Casa Milà waves and swells.
Rounded rooms cluster into a giant beehive.
Gaudí is turning nature into art.

He decorates chimneys on the roof,
a moving wonderland.
The rooftop courtyard looks like a ship.
Visitors feel rolling ocean waves beneath their feet.

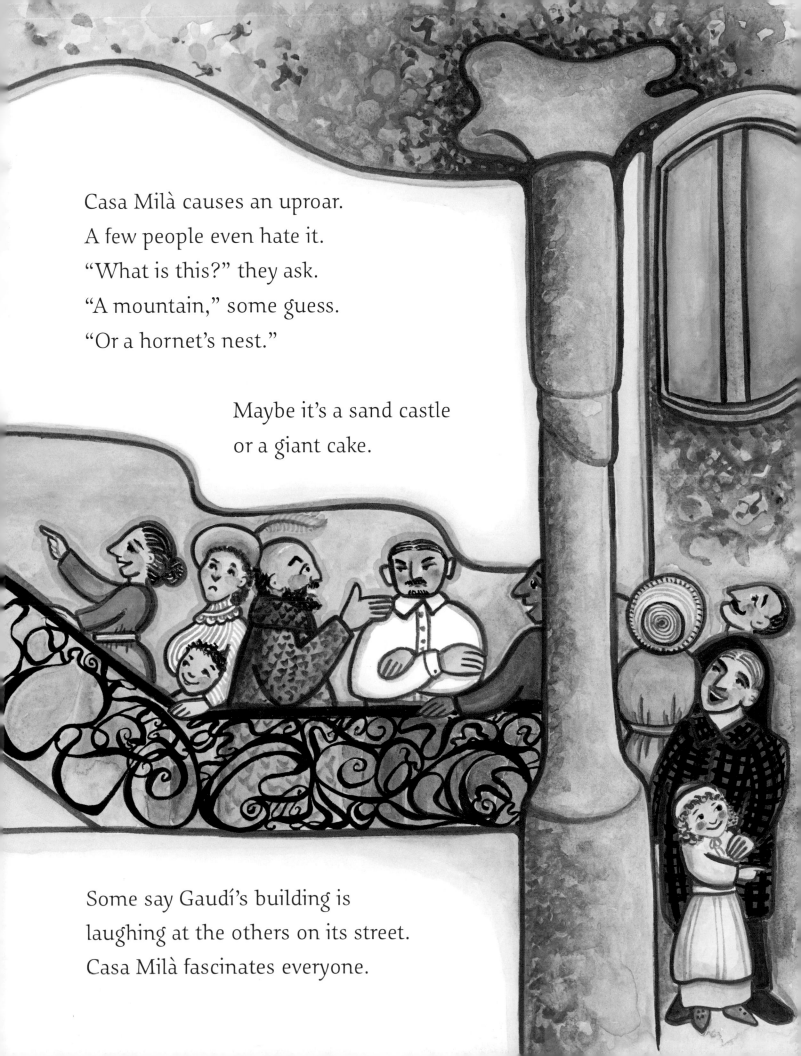

Casa Milà causes an uproar.
A few people even hate it.
"What is this?" they ask.
"A mountain," some guess.
"Or a hornet's nest."

Maybe it's a sand castle
or a giant cake.

Some say Gaudí's building is
laughing at the others on its street.
Casa Milà fascinates everyone.

Park Güell is a fantasyland set on a hillside.
Gatehouses warp and wave hello.
A mosaic lizard stands guard.

A long bench snakes around a playground.
Gaudí's workers smash old tiles, glass, and plates to bits.
They decorate the endless curving bench.
Gaudí praises his talented craftsmen.

Visitors pour in
to celebrate Gaudí's vision of Catalonia.

Gaudí grows older,
and still he works on
his Holy Family Church.
He uses the lessons
from all his other buildings
and dedicates his final
years to it.

Tile and Venetian glass
encrust soaring towers.
Inside, light filters through
a stone forest.

Gaudí's church shimmers like a dream over Barcelona.

Gaudí leaves
behind few words or plans.
His daring creations speak for him.
They tell his stories.
They are Gaudí's poem to the world.

Gaudí's buildings curve and arch.
They sparkle and glitter
and whisper with joy.

They stand waiting for you to
see with your very own eyes.

AUTHOR'S NOTE

ANTONI GAUDÍ i Cornet (ahn-TOH-nee gow-DEE ee KOR-net) was born on June 25, 1852, in southern Catalonia, Spain. The youngest of three children, Gaudí suffered from rheumatoid arthritis as a child. As a teenager, he expressed interest in art and architecture. He attended college in the city of Barcelona and learned from apprenticeships with established builders. Many in the region of Catalonia feel proud of their heritage and feel separate from the rest of Spain. Sharing that pride, Gaudí enjoyed weekend outings with a club to study Catalonia's historical sites.

Gaudí's early projects soon rejected the Gothic style's straight lines and confining symmetry. His tile work, arches, use of rubble, and lush planting reflect the influence of Mudejar style (mew-THE-haar, a Spanish hybrid of Moorish and Christian architecture). Gaudí embraced a new modern style known for its swirls and curving lines—*Modernisme*, or Art Nouveau. The movement's sometimes over-the-top curlicue glory prompted a French critic to call it "vermicelli in delirium."

Gaudí valued the talented artisans who collaborated with him on his works. A recycler ahead of his time, he and his workers broke old cups, wine bottles, and saucers to use in the mosaic detail of such works as Park Güell.

As his fame grew internationally, Gaudí was invited to draft sketches for a New York City skyscraper hotel. Unfortunately, the fabulous designs never came to life. Gaudí's startling modern works often inspired controversy—his bold innovation and departure from familiar forms caused many to debate the meaning of his work. La Sagrada Familia still generates questions about its appeal and whether it should be completed or left unfinished in his honor.

At the age of seventy-four in 1926, Gaudí was struck by a tram near Sagrada Familia and died days later. Thousands joined the funeral procession for a talented local son, genius, and folk hero. Taking inspiration from nature and his own Catholic faith, Gaudí created a new language for building.

Today, seven of Gaudí's buildings are UNESCO World Heritage Sites for creative contribution to the development of architecture and building technology. These structures are **Casa Vicens** (1883–1888); **Palacio Güell** (1885–1890); **Colonia Güell Crypt** (1898–1916); **Casa Batlló** (1904–1906); **Casa Milà** (1906–1910); **Park Güell** (1900-1914); and **La Sagrada Familia Nativity façade and Crypt** (1883–1926). Other structures that are mentioned in this book are the lampposts for **Plaça Reial**, City of Barcelona (1878–1880); the **Casa Calvet y Pinto** (1898–1900), which has the door knocker squashing the bug; and the Dragon gate at **Finca Güell** (1884–1887).

For many, Gaudí's works symbolize the eclectic, creative spirit of Barcelona and pride in Catalonian culture and heritage. Each year, countless visitors pay homage to Gaudí's boundless imagination and daring originality.

You can see photos of Gaudí's buildings on the Web sites listed below.

Barcelona Gaudí Architecture: www.barcelona-tourist-guide.com
The Barcelona of Antoni Gaudí: www.red2000.com
Gaudí & Barcelona Club: www.gaudiclub.com
Great Buildings Online: www.greatbuildings.com
Our Place, The World Heritage Collection: www.ourplaceworldheritage.com
World Heritage Site: www.worldheritagesite.org

SELECTED BIBLIOGRAPHY

Dalisi, Riccardo. *Gaudí: Furniture and Objects.* Woodbury, N.Y.: Barron's, 1980.
Martinell, César. *Gaudí: His Life, His Theories, His Work.* Cambridge, Mass.: MIT Press, 1975.
Nonell, Juan Bassegoda. *Antonio Gaudi: Master Architect.* New York: Abbeville Press, 2000.
Permanyer, Lluis. *Gaudí of Barcelona.* New York: Rizzoli International Publications, 1997.
Solà-Morales, Ignasi de. *Antoni Gaudí.* New York: Harry Abrams, 2003.
Van Hensbergen, Gijs. *Gaudí: A Biography.* New York: HarperCollins, 2001.